HILLEL SAID...

April 21, 1996
2 Iyar 5756

Dear Friends:

May the words of Hillel and Temple Hillel continue to inspire you for years to come.

With love from House to House.

*L*EARNING *is regarded by the sages as the duty of every Jew and as a basis of all useful and virtuous living.*

from "The Myth Maker" by Hyam Maccoby

For Evelyn Kravetz — who has followed Hillel with me.

HILLEL SAID...

COMMENTARY BY
NATHAN KRAVETZ

ILLUSTRATED BY
MANUEL BENNETT

A STUDENT SAYS... by *Allison Henteloff*

Joseph Simon / *Pangloss Press*
MALIBU, CALIFORNIA

ABOUT THE TYPES

The main text of this book was set in Monotype Centaur, Roman, Italic
and swash capitals; and each commentary begins with a Balle initial capital.

Composed by Greg Endries,
San Gabriel, California

*T*RUTH RESTS WITH GOD
ALONE — AND A LITTLE BIT WITH ME.

Yiddish Proverb

CONTENTS

ABOUT OUR CONTRIBUTORS

NATHAN KRAVETZ: A scholar and teacher who has long been immersed in Jewish history and culture, has researched Hillel's time, and has added his commentary. He received his doctoral degree in education at the University of California, Los Angeles. He has been an international consultant in education to governments in Europe, Asia, Africa, and South America. Dr. Kravetz received an All-University Fellowship at Harvard, and a Fulbright Senior Research Award for Argentina. He was Professor of Education at Hunter College, and Dean of the School of Education at the California State University in San Bernardino.

MANUEL BENNETT: After his service in the U.S. Army in World War II, he traveled to Mexico to continue his art studies with the Mexican great masters, and became a part of their renowned art colony. He is actively engaged in various disciplines of painting, sculpture and graphics. His work has been included in international exhibits for many years. He has contributed to the UNICEF Children's Fund, and has also produced many children's books for the Mexican school system. This is his fourth illustrated book for Pangloss Press. His last work on Sholem-Aleykhem's, "Tevye the Dairyman" is a companion volume to this book.

ALLISON HENTELOFF: As a young student at Hebrew Union College, she is in her third year, including her first year at Hebrew Union College in Jerusalem. She has also studied in France and Italy. It was the rabbis and scholars in Jewish studies who have moved Allison into her eventual commitment to become a rabbi. It is because Allison represents the emerging enthusiasm of young people toward the morality of Judaism that she eagerly wished to be a part of this focus on Hillel.

FOREWORD: THE HISTORY

of the Jewish people is enriched by a number of important teachers in whom we justly take pride. As we study the Torah in its written and oral forms, we honor the rabbis and scholars who have provided for us their comments and clarifications. Among them is Hillel, the great teacher who speaks to us even today.

We recall the dignity and worth of Akiva, Judah Ha-Nasi, the Geonim, Rashi, Judah Ha-Levi, Maimonides, Nahmanides, Joseph Karo, and many more. Rabbi Hillel was among those who were accorded the title, Nasi (Prince), for his noble character and celebrated teachings. Gentiles and Jews respect and honor the contributions of the wise men of Israel who expressed so well their understanding of Judaism. It is possible that Jesus, who was a Jew of the same period, knew of Rabbi Hillel and, acknowledging the wisdom of his famous reply to the pagan, spoke of it and taught it himself.

We must realize that during Hillel's time and after, there was much turmoil and strife in the Jewish world under the Roman Empire. Jews had hopes for the coming of the Messiah who had been promised to resolve their problems and bring God's kingdom to the world. In the meantime, they studied and learned with their rabbis. Jews in the time of the Second Temple respected the various Jewish thinkers as well as the pronouncements of the Sanhedrin, the council that met in the Temple as a court and a legislative body, headed by Hillel. Others of the populations under Roman rule put their faith and beliefs in the numerous gods and oracles who spoke some kind of "truth" in answer to their questions.

It was after the death of Jesus that some Jews, especially Paul, felt that a new religion should be established. Cherishing the Torah and the Talmud and the numerous commentaries of the

Rabbis, most Jews did not accept a new faith which broke with the Mosaic Law. They rejected Paul's teachings about Jesus as a supernatural being and they continued to reject the Christian gospels which were prepared well after the death of Jesus.

In Hillel the Jews had a teacher who was born in Babylonia among the Jews of exile. When he came to Jerusalem he was soon acclaimed as a brilliant rabbi. He was known to his colleagues as "Hillel the Babylonian," and was regarded as a wise and thoughtful scholar. They appreciated his ways of making clear the requirements of the Law and yet expressing a flexibility and warmth toward all who came to him to learn.

As a person, he was described as a humble man, of a kind disposition and honorable character. He considered all fellow Jews as his equal and he was willing to learn from them as well as teach. His students were always aware of his deep respect for Jewish Law and for them as willing learners. In his ethical and religious teachings, Hillel expressed his understanding both of the Law and of the needs of the Jews in the world they then inhabited.

Hillel's character and personality, which combined wisdom with humility and righteousness, became a model for the generations that followed his. His interpretations of the Law and his decisions have influenced Jews until this day.

It is appropriate, therefore, to offer to young people, ready to take their place in their communities, the heart and soul of Hillel. This book is our modest contribution to sharing what Hillel said in his time and continues to say to us today. Hillel's teachings should serve as a guide for all who wish to learn and welcome his wisdom.

by Nathan Kravetz

A STUDENT SAYS: *I* GREW UP in a secular home in Los Angeles, California. Though born of two Jewish parents—my mother, an athiest, and my father, a cynical agnostic—I did not find my Jewish connection in the home. When I was twelve years old, I wanted to have a bat-mitzvah, partly because many of my friends were having them and partly because I wanted to learn about who I was and from where I came. After much debate, my parents gave in and allowed me to have the ceremony and a modest party. I remained connected to the synagogue while my parents were unaffiliated. While I was in high school, the synagogue gave me a scholarship to attend UAHC (Union of American Hebrew Congregations) Kutz Camp in Warwick, New York. This high school leadership camp changed the way I interacted with the world. It was at Kutz where I was first introduced to many Jewish texts and scholars.

Among my favorites was Rabbi Hillel. His simple, yet profound wisdom touched the core of my being and opened up my heart and mind to the essence of Judaism. Rabbi Hillel and his followers taught about action, self-respect, compassion for others, and the power of knowledge. These are values after which I hope to model my life.

In the years that followed, I kept the message of Hillel's teachings, yet I did not continue my involvement in the Jewish youth movement. It wasn't until my sophomore year in college, when I was studying in both France and Italy, that my Jewish identity took a new leap. I was acutely aware of being the only Jew in my academic program. When I met other Jews who were traveling, I was so relieved. I felt an automatic sense of camaraderie and family ties. I can't really explain it, but it was at this time that I realized I was part of a much larger whole—the Jewish family.

9

The Torah refers to the people of Israel as Beit Yaakov (House of Jacob) or B'nei Ysrael (Children of Israel). All Jews come from the line of Jacob. Jacob's name was changed to Israel after struggling with the angel of G-d. We are all children of that struggle. Every Jew has wrestled with his or her Jewish identity in one way or another, whether it was when you were younger: "Mom, Dad, why do I have to go to Hebrew School?" Or as a teenager: "Why can't I date someone who's not Jewish?" Or throughout your life: "What does G-d have to do with me?"

As I became more involved with Jewish life on campus, my parents began to take another look at their Jewish identity. Through their support and encouragement of my struggles and exploration, they too became acquainted with Jewish thoughts and culture. After my junior year of college, I went to a program called BCI (Brandeis Collegiate Institute). This was a camp for young Jewish adults. I learned about the role of women in Judaism, the importance of the state of Israel to all Jewish people around the world, the history of the Jewish experience, Jewish mysticism, creative and traditional prayer, and much more. It was at BCI that I became reacquainted with the teachings of Rabbi Hillel. And again I was moved. Hillel's words resonated with my intellectual, psychological, and spiritual being. It was then that I realized the words in my heart: To learn more and embrace the teachings of our tradition. It was then that I decided to become a rabbi. I am currently a third year rabbinical student at the Hebrew Union College-Jewish Institute of Religion in New York.

"To the place that my heart loves, there do my feet lead me."

by Allison Henteloff

HILLEL SAID...

Your parents, your first teachers, will not shame you
when you are curious about the world.

HILLEL SAID: *A person too anxious about being shamed cannot learn.*

COMMENTARY: THERE is no shame if you don't know—only shame in refusing to learn. When you face your teacher, none of your questions should be considered stupid or foolish. Your parents, who are your first teachers, will not shame you when you are curious about the world. No one should cause you shame or suppress your interest in exploring that world. As a true learner, without anxiety, you sit at the feet of the true teacher.

When you seek knowledge for yourself, you enrich those around you.

HILLEL SAID: *He who increases Torah increases life.*

COMMENTARY: FOR JEWS, Torah is learning, knowledge, and truth. It is our Bible. When you seek knowledge for yourself, you enrich those around you and provide truth for your family and community. The beginning of learning and knowledge is Torah, a never-ending source of truth.

Without the sages we lose our place in the world.

HILLEL SAID: *He who does not attend upon the sages deserves reproach.*

COMMENTARY: THE teachers with whom you learn deserve the full attention of your eyes, your ears, and your hearts. To learn from these sages is to understand the past and the present. Without the sages we lose our place in the world. The words of the sages are like seeds upon fertile ground, planting for the learner's future.

Hillel wrote severely, emphasizing in this way the respect and attention that we should give to the wise.

Fame created of exaggeration is made of air.

HILLEL SAID: *A name made great is a name destroyed.*

COMMENTARY: FAME creates the creatures you see as large, powerful, and somehow important. Such names are blown up, exaggerated, built on air, getting "fifteen minutes of fame." No matter how great such individuals may appear, in them you find little of love, or thought, or meaning. They are carried away with their self-importance. The destruction of a name thus made great is inevitable, while you as a learner stand firm without concern for "greatness."

And those quiet fields away from all others.

HILLEL SAID: *To the place that my heart loves, there do my feet lead me.*

COMMENTARY: HILLEL spoke in this way of his devotion to the House of Study and to the Temple in Jerusalem of his day. So you may find places that your heart loves: your home, your parents, your family, your own house of study, and those quiet fields away from all others where you may indulge your joy in God's creation. To all such places, your feet should lead you willingly.

Pride, honors, power remove us from God and humanity.

HILLEL SAID: *My humiliation is my exaltation, my exaltation is my humiliation.*

COMMENTARY: PRIDE, honors, power—all such exaltations remove us from God and humanity. When your own honest reflection removes the cloak of pride, the crown of honors, and the scepter of power, you are free of false garb and in this exaltation you are now closer to your God, to your people, and to truth.

The unwise want the sun to rise and set only on themselves.

HILLEL SAID: *If I am not for myself, who will be for me? And if I am only for myself, what am I? And if not now, when?*

COMMENTARY: AT EVERY possible moment, you are required to declare yourself; but not to serve your own needs only. You must stand for your own principles as you have learned justice and wisdom. Such knowledge must be offered unselfishly, for others as well as for yourself. When do you act? It must be now and it cannot be put off to a time that may never come. In our society, the unwise want the sun to rise and set only on themselves. For each of us the road is ours to choose.

A pagan asked Hillel to teach him the Law while
he stood on one leg.

HILLEL SAID: *What is hateful to you, never do to your neighbor: that is the entire Torah; all the rest is commentary. Now go forth and learn.*

COMMENTARY: HILLEL has given to his Jewish family and community the single guideline by which all people should live. Still, he says, you are required to study throughout your life and so to grow in tolerance and understanding.

To yearn after fame is to lose the reason you have it: your own true self.

HILLEL SAID: *He who advertises his name, loses it.*

COMMENTARY: THE INFLATED self-importance shown by some is pompous and ridiculous. As you gain in knowledge and understanding, you will be accepted by those around you. You will offer your gains to them for their benefit. You need not seek praise or renown for your greater accomplishments. To yearn after fame is to lose the reason you have it: your own true self.

You cannot see the world through another's eyes.

HILLEL SAID: *Do not judge your neighbor until you are in his place.*

COMMENTARY: YOUR FRIEND acts for himself or herself, surely with thoughtfulness and good judgment. You may question your friend's acts but you cannot see the world through another's eyes. The question remains: is he still your friend? And that you must decide for yourself, thoughtfully, avoiding the evil of gossip.

Do what is needed to turn swords into ploughshares.

HILLEL SAID: *Be among the disciples of Aaron, loving peace, and pursuing peace, loving humanity and bringing them closer to the Torah.*

COMMENTARY: WHEN PEACE is only an abstract word it is shallow and meaningless. You must remember the main elements of Judaism: peace and pursuit of peace, love for mankind, and the truth and wisdom of the Torah. These are the goals and purposes of your efforts in life. All humanity—Jew and non-Jew alike—can accept the power and value in Hillel's command and do what is needed to turn swords into ploughshares.

A *mentsh* is a decent and honest person.

HILLEL SAID: *In the place where there are no men, strive to be a man.*

COMMENTARY: *T*HOUGH Yiddish was not spoken in Hillel's time, he taught that it is necessary to be a *mentsh*. What is a *mentsh?* Simply a decent, honest person who offers gentleness and kindness, in both thought and action. You are a man or a woman, but a *mentsh* you must be. Where there are none, be one, he said.

Your possessions are not you.

HILLEL SAID: *The more possessions, the more anxiety.*

COMMENTARY: IF YOU load yourself down with things, your fears and concerns are focused on them: their price, their condition, their usefulness. But you have them for only a short time. Your possessions are not you. The most important things you can own are learning and knowledge, wisdom and compassion. These are the true values of a man or woman. They will never grow old or wear out, and they will serve you and yours without anxiety wherever you may go.

Each of your congregations gives you strength.

HILLEL SAID: *Do not separate from the congregation.*

COMMENTARY: *Y*OU BELONG to several congregations and communities where you are an important member: your family, your school, your cherished friends. Each congregation encourages you and gives you strength. You will never labor alone when you stand within your congregations and serve the needs of all.

The righteous are those with compassion for others.

HILLEL SAID: *The more righteousness, the more peace.*

COMMENTARY: PEACE REQUIRES that all who desire it should be righteous. Who are the righteous? Those who have compassion for others, who study and learn the wisdom of those who came before, and who offer true wisdom and compassion for the sake of peace. Such must be the way of nations and of each of us.

Respect your body; do not disfigure or damage it.

HILLEL SAID: *It is a mitzvah (a worthy act) to keep one's body clean. If the statues of the kings are washed and scrubbed, how much more should we, created in the image of God, take care of our bodies.*

COMMENTARY: YOU CARE for your body not only with cleanliness and bathing, but by keeping it free of dangerous substances and of preventable disease and pain. You do not disfigure your body and so invite the dangers of injury, disrespect, and the falling away from wisdom. How many are desperate for health who have spurned it for too long! What is the use of pursuing only vanity and bodily pleasures?

Each stage in your life supports the next.

HILLEL SAID: *He who does not increase his knowledge, decreases it.*

COMMENTARY: YOU CANNOT stand still and say, "I'm done." Learning is a life-long experience, now more than ever. To seek knowledge, wisdom, and understanding keeps you from growing smaller. Each stage in your life leads to the next and calls for your gaining wisdom as you follow it. So you earn the full measure and pleasure of life!

You are not expected to imitate those who lead you from your chosen path.

HILLEL SAID: *Among those who stand, do not sit; among those who sit, do not stand. Among those who weep, do not laugh.*

COMMENTARY: *T*HROUGHOUT your life you are required to respect the wisdom and knowledge of those around you. You are not expected to imitate slavishly or join thoughtlessly with those whose standing, sitting, or weeping may offend you or lead you from your own chosen path. It is for you only to choose when to oppose, when to approve, and when to stand forcefully alone. You are called upon, finally, to be true to yourself.

Charity offers an open-handed love for others.

HILLEL SAID: *He who increases charity, increases peace.*

COMMENTARY: ALL HUMANKIND yearns for the peace that nourishes the lives of individuals and of peoples. When you extend your hand with a portion of what you have and give freely in kindness and love, you establish peace. Thus, charity is not an expression of self-love, but of open-handed love for others in the spirit of peace.

He who does good, feels good.

HILLEL SAID: *He who increases his good deeds is establishing peace within his own body.*

COMMENTARY: HE WHO does good, feels good. When you go further than ever in your charity, your loving kindness, and your search for truth, you earn the benefits of peace of mind, continuing satisfaction, and confidence to go forward.

Hillel esteems his wife for all she is and does as
a woman, as his wife and equal partner.

HILLEL SAID: *"I judge you in the scale of merit, that all your deeds are for the sake of heaven,"* [He said to his wife.]

COMMENTARY: HILLEL esteems his wife for all she is and does as a woman, as his wife and equal partner. Her deeds are her expression of her charity and love of learning. They are done not only for herself and her family, but for her continuing connection with God.

You are not expected to follow others blindly.

HILLEL SAID: *When others are gathering,
scatter; when others are scattering, gather.*

COMMENTARY: YOU ARE reminded
that you must observe with thoughtful
judgment what others are doing and say-
ing. You are not expected to follow blindly,
but to let your own knowledge and wisdom guide you. Can you do the opposite
of what others are doing? Often, that is
exactly what you must do and what would
be best for you and yours. Fashions
change, and today's fashion will be gone
tomorrow.

In time, others will recognize the value of your wisdom.

HILLEL SAID: *If no one is buying, buy!*

COMMENTARY: ƮO DO whatever others do is to move with the flow of the stream, to blow with whatever winds may blow. If no one is buying—an idea, a product, a set of values—you may find the one you want to "buy" and make it your own. In time, others will recognize the value of your choice and will seek you out. Your ideas will be seen as worthwhile for others to "buy."

We teach all of humanity who surround us.

HILLEL SAID: *Teach all men.*

COMMENTARY: WE EMPHASIZE the word TEACH, which means to offer what we have of our stock of knowledge. We stress ALL, and we leave no one aside without our help. We say strongly, MEN, and we mean all of humanity who surround us and require teaching that leads to goodness and peace.

You must think carefully before you speak.

HILLEL SAID: *Do not say something that cannot be understood because you think that, in the end, it will be understood.*

COMMENTARY: AS YOU reach out with your words to those who face you, you need to understand who and what they are. You must think carefully before you speak. Your words must be complete, leaving nothing to be guessed or imagined, or you have said nothing at all. Deal with your friends honestly and completely and you will ensure your friends' learning and your common peace.

When you judge harshly, you drive away friendship.

HILLEL SAID: *Be patient and thoughtful in judging and rebuking.*

COMMENTARY: THE BEST friend, and the best teacher, is the one who is concerned about another's feelings. When you judge someone harshly and severely you drive away friendship and the interest in learning from you. Rebuking, scolding, and "putting down" are the opposite of the patience and kindness on which friendships live.

We welcome the friend as well as the stranger.

HILLEL SAID: *When someone comes to join you, reach out both hands to bring him close to the Torah.*

COMMENTARY: WE WELCOME the friend as well as the stranger with kindness and good will. The one who wants to join you wants to share your friendship, to follow your path, to learn with you, and to gain your respect and love. To reach out toward another brings you both closer to humanity and to God.

Be ready to answer anger with the strength of reason.

HILLEL SAID: *Be patient and humble, not easy to anger.*

COMMENTARY: BE NOT easy to anger, but be ready to answer anger with strength: the strength of reason, of good will, of patience and respect. You can have good reason for anger on behalf of a good cause and against injustice. The justice of your cause should bring forth the strength of others who will join you in the same fight.

You cannot offer your values to others if you are
impatient or angry.

HILLEL SAID: *An irritable person cannot teach.*

COMMENTARY: *Y*OU CANNOT bring to others the benefits of your knowledge and wisdom if you are impatient, unpleasant, and angry. Nor can you bring love to another or expect it back. In your words and your actions, you succeed with kindness and gentleness, and with your interest in the well-being of those who come to you to learn.

Your love of learning is the same as your love of
mankind.

HILLEL SAID: *Become learned out of love and not out of severity.*

COMMENTARY: WHEN YOU approach learning and knowledge with willing enthusiasm, you gain both the essence of the Law and its applications. A rigid teacher, overly stiff and formal, will drive away the learner. Your love of learning is the same as your love of mankind; you offer openness to others' ideas, to different approaches, to unexpected but reasonable answers. All are natural to the devoted friend and eager learner.

You live every day the meanings of the blessings.

HILLEL SAID: *Blessed is the Lord, today —*
and every day.

COMMENTARY: WE CELEBRATE the traditions of our people not only on one day of the week, or during one week of the year. As you bless the Lord and yourself, you live each and every day the meanings of the blessings and reflect upon them. In your daily words and actions, you express yourself continously as a just and honorable human being.

The wise person may be found anywhere in the community.

HILLEL SAID: *Not everyone who is much engaged in business becomes wise.*

COMMENTARY: WE CHOOSE our work to satisfy our needs, our interests, and our souls. Wisdom is needed to prepare us for work in any field. All work is worthy of the worker, whether it brings wealth or not. The wise person may be found anywhere in the community, and can gain for us the benefits of a worthy and wise worker, regardless of wealth.

To give wise and thoughtful counsel is to enrich
the giver.

HILLEL SAID: *The more counsel, the more understanding.*

COMMENTARY: WHEN YOU receive advice and suggestions from a wise person—a friend, a teacher, or a family member—you gain for yourself the values that will guide you in life. It is also true that to give wise and thoughtful counsel is to enrich the giver who sees and understands the needs of another. The one who offers good counsel is to be respected and cherished.

Time does count.

HILLEL SAID: *Do not say, "When I'll have time, I'll study." Perhaps you will never have any time.*

COMMENTARY: FOR HILLEL, a good act is to study and learn, to gain wisdom. All such good acts should be done, not when you will have time, but as soon as you know what needs to be done. Keep an eye on the calendar and on the clock. Time does indeed count. You cannot postpone what is necessary, for yourself or for others.

Your good name stands for justice and honor.

HILLEL SAID: *He who has acquired a good name, has gained it for himself.*

COMMENTARY:　YOUR GOOD name stands for justice and honor, and for your kindness and wisdom. These are the qualities that establish your standing in the community. You have gained it for yourself, and whether it's in big lights or in large print does not matter. It is not for yourself alone. How will you share that good name with those who depend upon you: your family, your community, your people?

Riches are useless until you reach out to offer.

HILLEL SAID: *He who makes his own use of the crown shall perish.*

COMMENTARY: WHEN YOU have
reached the height of your powers, of your
wisdom, and of your sense of responsibility
you must look about you. Such riches that
are yours are useless unless you reach out
to offer and share with those who do not
yet have the "crown," or who may never
reach it. Thus you are wiser and your life
is made even richer.

If you offer nothing of yourself, you are truly absent.

HILLEL SAID: *If I am here, all are here. If I am not here, who is here?*

COMMENTARY: WHEN YOU join in the work of your family and your friends, you add your strength and your wisdom to make each task lighter. With you, all are strengthened. If you offer nothing of yourself, you are truly absent, and your community lacks needed substance and power.

In every group, each one has the power to contribute.

HILLEL SAID: *The least among you is a father of wisdom and will be a father of generations. As to the greatest among you, how much more so!*

COMMENTARY: IN EVERY group you will find some who are strong, and some who are weak. Yet each one has the power to contribute, and even the weak can come to wisdom and be the first of generations. Your own weaknesses can be overcome and bring you to knowledge and understanding. Now, if you are already strong in wisdom, you can become learned even sooner and more deeply, and bring greater strengths to your family and your people.

Reach out with love for others.

HILLEL SAID: *The love of God must be expressed through the love of fellowmen.*

COMMENTARY: ALL YOUR piety and all your devotion to God are meaningful only when you express them in your love and devotion to those around you. Your fellow men and women are those with whom you share the strength of your religious faith and actions. God needs no rituals, blessings, or prayers unless you reach out as well with love for others.

The windbag is soon dismissed as a laughingstock.

HILLEL SAID: *Say little and do much.*

COMMENTARY: DO YOU talk big and do nothing? Are you known as only a promiser? If so, you will receive little respect or admiration, and no followers. A windbag is soon dismissed as a laughingstock. When you carry out your promises in acts, your value for yourself and others becomes great. The greatest acts are best done with the fewest words.

The essence of living is to continue to learn.

HILLEL SAID: *Do not trust in yourself until your last day.*

COMMENTARY: THE ESSENCE of living is to continue to learn and to gain in knowledge, understanding, and wisdom. You may be confident that tomorrow will bring you to even greater heights of accomplishment. Across the years, as you grow in your own powers, you remember those others who provided you with support and encouragement. You are never alone.

Listen to the thoughts of Hillel. They now belong
to you.

... AND THE SAGES SAID: *A person should always be like Hillel.*

COMMENTARY: *W*HAT YOU have thought and read here were the thoughts and wisdom of our teacher, Hillel. Now they belong to you.

SUGGESTED ADDITIONAL READING

Buxbaum, Yitzhak: *The Life and Teachings of Hillel*, New Jersey: Aronson, 1994.

Falk, Harvey: *Jesus the Pharisee. A New Look at the Jewishness of Jesus*, New York: Paulist Press, 1985.

Gilbert, Martin, ed.: *Atlas of Jewish Civilization*, New York: Macmillan, 1990.

Hilberg, Raul: *Perpetrators, Victims, Bystanders, The Jewish Catastrophe 1933-1945*, New York: Harper Collins, 1992.

Kolatch, Alfred J.: *The Jewish Book of Why*, New York: Jonathan David, 1981.

Maccoby, Hyam, ed.: *The Day God Laughed*, New York: St. Martin's Press, 1978.

Maccoby, Hyam: *The Mythmaker: Paul and the Invention of Christianity*, New York: Harper, 1986.

Potok, Chaim: *Wanderings. Chaim Potok's History of the Jews*, New York: Alfred A. Knopf, 1978.

Roth, Cecil: *History of the Jews*, New York: Schocken, 1971.

Wouk, Herman: *This is My God*, New York: Doubleday, 1959.